It was Saturday. Kim and Sam were going
"I'm off, Mum!" yelled Kim.
"Wait!" said Mum. "I've got lots to do to
with you."

"Oh Mum, no!" said Kim. "They'll spoil it."
"Oh Kim, yes!" said Mum. "They won't spoil it. And keep your eye on them, OK?"
"OK," sighed Kim. "Come on, you two."

The twins pulled Sam and Kim along the street.
"I want sweets!" yelled Jenny.
"I want sweets, too!" yelled Ben.
"OK," sighed Kim. "Come on, you two. Let's go to Sid's Sweet Stall."

They went to Sid's Sweet Stall. Fred the Fiddle was next to the stall. He was a friend of Sam's dad.

"Hello, Sam!" said Fred the Fiddle.

"Hello, Fred!" said Sam.

4

Then Jenny squealed.
"Oo! Look!" she said.
"Oo! Oo! Look! Look!" squealed Ben.
"Oh no," sighed Kim. "Puppies!"
"Puppies!" squealed Jenny and Ben.

The puppies were next to a big, green van. The twins pulled Kim and Sam over to the van.
"Look! Puppies!" shouted Jenny.
"Look! Puppies!" shouted Ben.
"Oh, you two!" sighed Kim.

There were two men by the puppies. Another man sat in the green van.
The puppies were in small cages. The cages were really, really small.

"Sweet little puppies – look at them play!" one of the men called.
"Sweet little puppies – must go today!" called another man.
"I want this puppy!" yelled Jenny.
"I want this puppy!" yelled Ben.
"*No puppies*!" yelled Kim. "Come on, you two."

"Wait, Kim," said Sam. He looked really cross.
"What's up?" said Kim.
"Look at the cages! They're too small," said Sam. "It isn't right."
"What can we do?" said Kim.

"Wait here," said Sam. "I'm going to talk to Fred. He'll know what to do."
He ran back to Sid's Sweet Stall to find Fred.

Sam told Fred about the puppies.

"Right," said Fred. "I know those three men. They're up to no good. I'm going to call the police."

In no time at all, a police car raced up to the market.

"Police!" yelled the man in the van.
The other men pushed the puppies into the van and raced off.
"Oh no!" yelled Kim. "Where are the twins?"

Sam and Kim looked all over the market but they could not find Jenny and Ben.
"Oh no!" said Kim. "Mum will kill me! She told me to keep an eye on them."

"Hello, Kim," said Fred. "What's up?"
"We've lost the twins!" said Kim.
"Where did you see them last?" said Fred.
"By the van!" said Sam.
"Oh no! They might have got into that van," said Kim. "What shall we do?"

They had to tell Kim's mum and dad.
Kim's dad called the police straight away.
"We've got the men, the van and the puppies," said the policeman, "but the twins aren't in the van."
"Then where are they?" said Kim's dad. "Where are they?"

"We'll look for them straight away," said the policeman.
"We'll all help," everyone said.
"I'll get Info-rider," said Sam.

Sam jumped onto Info-rider.
"Come on, Kim!" he shouted. "We'll find the twins."

Sam and Kim raced to the hill.
"Put on the tracker!" said Kim.
"OK!" said Sam.
"Tracker on – tracker on," flashed the screen.

They met Fred by the stream. He was with his dog, Rex. "Rex is tracking the twins by sniffing," said Fred. "He's a good sniffer!"

They looked and looked. Rex sniffed and sniffed. Then Info-rider's screen began to flash.
"Look in the bushes! Look in the bushes!" it said.

They all went over to the bushes. Rex began to bark and bark.
"I bet they are in there!" said Kim.
Rex pushed his way into the bushes.

Out from the bushes came Rex, then Ben, then Jenny and then…
a puppy!
"They've got a puppy!" said Kim.
"They've got one of the puppies from the market," said Sam.
"It's *our* puppy," said Ben.

Just then Kim's mum and dad came up with the policeman.
"We've been looking for you two all over the place," said Mum.
"Where has that puppy come from?" said Dad.
"It's one of the puppies from the market," said Kim.

"What a sweet little puppy!" said Mum.
"Can we keep it?" said Dad.
"Why not? It needs a good home," said the policeman.
"Hurray!" said Jenny.
"Hurray!" said Ben.
"Oh, you two!" sighed Kim.